INDONESIAN

exotic dishes from empal daging to nasi goreng for
creative cooking

REBO
PUBLISHERS

Foreword

Indonesian cooking is a big adventure, which begins with colorful, exotic, and strange ingredients. This leads to oriental stores and along unknown paths to the ethnic foods section of the supermarket. Even if there is no Indonesian community in your neighborhood, almost all the ingredients can be found at Thai, Chinese, or Indian grocery stores, and you can also obtain them by mail order. Be adventurous, if you like southeast Asian food, you will love Indonesian cuisine. On pages 6 and 7 you will find a list of the main ingredients and explanations as to how they taste and where to find them. With this acquired knowledge, you will be able to plunge into the unknown, at first hesitantly, but you'll soon get the hang of it. You'll love Indonesian food from the first bite!

There is so much to discover: From Sajoer Loddeh (Vegetables in Coconut Milk) and Ajam Aoreng (Spicy Chicken Croquettes) to Bubuh Injin (Black Rice Pudding).

INDONESIAN

Colophon

© 2003 Rebo International b.v., Lisse, The Netherlands

www.rebo-publishers.com - info@rebo-publishers.com

Original recipes and photographs © R&R Publishing Pty. Ltd.

Design, editing, production and Typesetting:

Minkowsky Graphics Bureau, Enkhuizen, The Netherlands

Adaptation and editing: American Pie, London, UK and Sunnyvale, California, USA

ISBN 90 366 1471 6

Contents

page 6	Indonesian ingredients
8	appetizers
18	noodles and rice
28	meat
40	fish and seafood
54	poultry
70	vegetables
86	desserts

Assem djawa (tamarind)—This gives a sour flavor to food. It is sold in blocks. To use it, cut off a piece and soak it in water. It is easier to use tamarind concentrate which is sold in jars in oriental and specialty stores.

Banana leaves—These can be bought from Chinese and other oriental stores. Banana leaves are steamed, to soften them and used to wrap food which is then steamed in them. If banana leaves are not available, wrap the food in aluminum foil.

Beans—The favorite beans in Indonesia are the Scarlet Runner or French bean, as well as the so-called yard-long beans. Fresh green beans and snap beans are available in supermarkets at any time of year.

Candlenut— A round nut rather like a macadamia that can be bought in most oriental grocer stores. If candlenuts are called for in a recipe and you don't have any, use macadamias or almonds.

Coconut milk (santen)—In Indonesia, fresh coconuts are often used in cooking. Coconut milk can be bought in cans or in powdered form for cooking. Make sure the coconut milk you use has not been sweetened.

Curry leaves—These spicy leaves gave curry its name. They are used to flavor foods in the same way as salam leaves. Buy them at Indian and oriental grocery stores

Indonesian ingredients

Daoen djeroek poeroet (kaffir lime leaves)—These glossy, dark-green, citrus leaves should be chopped in order to release their fragrance. They can be bought at oriental fruit and vegetable stores. Store the leaves in plastic bags in the deep freeze.

Daoen pandan (pandanus or screwpine leaves)—This leaf is added to stews and curries to give them a delicious fragrance. It can be bought at specialty oriental stores. Pandanus (screwpine) extract is also sometimes available. Use it sparingly.

Jaggery (palm sugar)—Hard, round pieces of reddish-brown sugar. Can be bought from Indian and other oriental grocery stores. If you cannot get it, substitute muscovado sugar or piloncillo, Mexican brown sugar.

Ketjap manis—Sweet soy sauce, available in ethnic supermarkets or specialty stores. This and another Indonesian dipping sauce, are typical Indonesian foods that are hard to find elsewhere.

Ketoembar (coriander)—In Indonesian cooking, the coriander (cilantro) seeds are used extensively, as well as the green leaves and stalks.

Koenjit (turmeric)—Turmeric belongs to the ginger family. You can find fresh turmeric root at Asian and especially Indian grocery stores. Ground turmeric is available in the spice section of any supermarket.

Laos (galingale)—Laos powder or galingale is a mild variety of ginger. You can find it fresh, dried or powdered at oriental grocery stores.

Lombok (chili peppers)—Indonesian cooking is spicy, and uses a lot of small red chili peppers, such as the birdseye chili pepper as well as large bell peppers. When handling chili peppers, always wear rubber gloves.

Salam leaves—Buy them dried from specialty stores or oriental grocery stores. They are used like bayleaves in Indonesian cookery.

Sambal oelek—Spicy paste much used in Indonesian cookery. Buy it at oriental grocery stores and some supermarkets.

Sereh (lemongrass)—Sereh (lemongrass) is the Indonesian substitute for the lemon flavor. Lemons do not grow in the wet heat of Indonesia, limes and kalamansi (sour orange) are the main sour citrus fruits. Fresh sereh is an important ingredient in the paste called boemboe served with fish dishes.It is fragrant and slightly sour.

Tempeh–Compressed, fermented soybean curd. Available from health food stores

Terasi (shrimp paste)–Trassi or terasi is sold in block or in powdered form. Cut off a small piece of the block to add to a dish, only a very small amount is needed. Do not be put off by the pungent smell. Keep the rest wrapped in foil. Trassi is an important ingredient in fish dishes. Buy it at oriental groceries..

Indonesian ingredients

Method

Make a pancake batter by mixing the flour with the, egg yolks, water, and salt in a bowl.

Heat a little oil in an omelet pan or skillet and add a little of the batter. Make the pancakes one by one. Leave the to drain on kitchen paper.

Heat more oil in a big saucepan, to make the filling. Add the onion, garlic, and ground beef and cook 2-3 minutes, stirring constantly until lightly browned. Then add the chili powder, ketjap manis, and cabbage, and cook for another 2-3 minutes. Leave the filling to cool.

Spread each pancake with a tablespoon of filling. Wrap up each pancake like a burrito, to keep the filling firmly inside. Pour the bread crumbs into a shallow dish and roll these filled pancakes in them to coat them.

Heat more oil in a skillet and sauté these croquettes for 1-2 minutes, turning frequently, until they are golden-brown and crunchy.
Drain them on kitchen paper and serve warm.

Ingredients

1⅓ cups/165g/5¾ oz all-purpose flour

2 eggs, separated

2 cups/500ml/18fl oz water

pinch of salt

¼ cup/2oz/50g dry bread crumbs

peanut oil

Begedel daging—Beef Croquettes

For the filling

1 tbsp/15ml peanut oil

1 brown onion, minced

2 garlic cloves, peeled

1¾ cups/14oz/400g ground beef

1-2 tsp/5-10g chili powder

1 tbsp/15ml ketjap manis

2 cups/250g/8oz shredded cabbage

Method

Combine the corn, lombok chili pepper, green onions, coriander, salt, egg, and sifted flour to make a batter. **Heat** enough oil to come 3in/7.5cm up the side of a wok or skillet.

Drop tablespoons of the batter into the pan and cook them, turning occasionally, until they are golden brown on both sides.

Serve the perkedel djagoeng with soy sauce.

Perkedel jagung—Corn Fritters

Ingredients

1¾ cups/14oz/400g canned corn, drained

1 small red chili pepper, deseeded and finely chopped

4 green shallots, sliced

1 tsp/5g ground coriander

pinch of salt

1 egg

3tbsp/1½oz/40 g all-purpose flour

vegetable oil for frying

Method

Crush or pound together shallots, garlic, and cumin seeds in a mortar with a pestle or in a small food processor.

Combine shallots with beef, bread crumbs, egg yolk, sambal oelek, and soy sauce. Shape mixture into small walnut-sized balls.

Heat the oil in a large skillet. Fry meatballs for 5-6 minutes or until cooked through and golden.

Serve meatballs with wedges of lime.

Rempah Daging—Spicy Meatballs

Ingredients

2 shallots, chopped

2 garlic cloves, chopped

1 tsp cumin seeds

1 tsp ground coriander

500g beef mince

3/4 cup fresh breadcrumbs

1 egg yolk

2 tsp sambal oelek

1 tbsp soy sauce

2 tbsp peanut oil

appetizers

13

Method

Combine shallots, garlic, ginger, fish, soy sauce, brown sugar, and egg in a food processor. Process until mixture is a smooth paste.

Using wet hands, shape mixture into small patties. (Mixture tends to be wet). Dip patties in cornstarch.

Heat oil in a skillet or wok. Cook fish cakes for 1-2 minutes on each side or until golden.

Combine ingredients for dipping sauce in a small dish. Serve fish cakes with dipping sauce.

Ingredients

4 green onions, chopped

2 garlic cloves, minced

2 tbsp/30g chopped ginger

1¼lb/500 g skinless white fish fillet

1 tbsp/15ml soy sauce,

1 tsp/5g brown sugar

1 egg

3 tbsp/1½oz/40g cornstarch

peanut oil for frying

Perkedel Ikan—Spicy Fish Fritters

Dipping Sauce

1 tbsp/15ml ketjap manis

2 tbsp/30ml soy sauce

½ tsp/2.5ml sambal oelek

Method

Preheat oven to 400°F/200°C. Lightly grease or spray a nonstick roasting pan with oil.Combine cornstarch, pepper, salt, coriander, cumin and chili powder in a mixing bowl. Toss chicken in cornstarch mixture to coat.

Place chicken in roasting pan, spray lightly with oil, and roast for 15-20 minutes or until golden and crisp.

Serve with ketjap manis or sambal oelek.

Ayam Goreng—
Spicy Chicken Drumettes

Ingredients

500g/1¼lb chicken drumsticks

1 cup/4oz/125g cornstarch

2 tsp/10g ground black pepper

½ tsp/2.5g salt

2 tsp/10g ground cumin

1 tsp/5g ground chili powder

Method

Boil the rice in boiling salted water for 10-12 minutes or until cooked. Drain and rinse.

Heat 2 tsp/10ml oil in a wok. Add the beaten egg and and swirl to coat the wok to form an omelet. Turn omelet and cook the other side. Remove and cut omelet into thin strips.

Heat remaining oil in wok. Add green onions, garlic, and chili and cook 1-2 minutes. Add chicken and stir-fry for 3 minutes. Add carrot, cabbage, shrimp, ketjap manis, and soy sauce. Stir-fry until cabbage wilts.

Add rice to mixture and stir-fry until heated through.

Serve rice with strips of omelet, fried onion-and-garlic mixture, and sambal oelek as a dipping sauce.

Ingredients

1¾ cups/14oz400g long-grain rice, washed

1½ tbsp/20ml peanut oil

2 eggs, beaten

4 green onions, finely chopped

2 garlic cloves, crushed

2 small lombok chili peppers, seeded and chopped

2 cups/10½oz/300g chicken breast, diced

Nasi goreng—Fried Rice

noodles and rice

2 cups shredded Chinese (Napa) cabbage

⅓ cup/3½oz/100g peeled shrimp

2-3 tbsp/30-45ml ketjap manis

1 tbsp/15ml soy sauce

Method

Cook noodles following package directions. Drain noodles and reserve them.

Heat the oil in a wok. Add shallots and cook until golden. Add chicken and garlic and stir-fry for 2 minutes. Add carrots and stir-fry for a further 2 minutes.

Add cabbage and ketjap manis and continue to cook until cabbage is wilted.

Add chicken broth, noodles, beansprouts, and green onions. Stir fry until heated through.

Bami goreng—Fried Noodles

Ingredients

7oz/200g egg noodles or vermicelli	2 cups/8oz/250g Chinese (Napa) cabbage, shredded
1 tbsp/15ml peanut oil	
1¼lb/500g chicken thighs, boned and diced	2 tbsp/30ml ketjap manis
4 shallots, sliced	⅓ cup/3½fl oz/100ml chicken broth
2 garlic cloves, crushed	1 cup/8oz/250g beansprouts
1 carrot, peeled and finely sliced	4 green onions (scallions), sliced

Method

Heat oil in a large stainless steel saucepan. Add turmeric, coriander, cumin, and rice. Stir for 1 minute to coat rice and cook until fragrant.
Add coconut milk, water, curry leaf, and cinnamon stick and bring to the boil. Reduce heat to low and cook for 10–12 minutes or until liquid is absorbed. Transfer rice to a steamer or rice-cooker* and steam rice for 10–12 minutes or until grains are light.

*If you don't have a steamer or rice-cooker, remove saucepan from heat, cover, and leave to stand for 10 minutes. Remove curry leaf and cinnamon stick and serve immediately.

Tip

This rice is traditionally served on special occasions.

Ingredients

1 tbsp/15ml vegetable oil

1 tsp/5g ground turmeric

1 tsp/5g ground coriander

½ tsp ground cumin

1¾ cups/14oz/400 g long-grain rice, washed

Nasi kuning—Yellow Rice

2 cups/16fl oz/500ml coconut milk

1 cup/8fl oz/250ml water

4 curry leaves

1 cinnamon stick

Method

Crush or pound ingredients for paste in a mortar and pestle or food processor. Heat extra oil in a saucepan. Add paste and stir-fry for 1–2 minutes.

Add turmeric and cumin and stir until aromatic. Add coconut milk, chicken broth, brown sugar, broccoli, cauliflower, and carrot. Bring to the boil, reduce heat, and cover the pan.

Cook for 6-8 minutes or until vegetables are tender. Stir in noodles and serve.

Sayur kari—Vegetables Curry

Ingredients

Paste

1 garlic clove, minced

1 shallot, minced

1 medium chili, deseeded and chopped

4 tsp/20ml peanut oil

½ tsp/2.5g ground turmeric

1 tsp/5g ground cumin

¼ cup/2fl oz/60ml coconut milk (santen)

1 cup/8fl oz/250ml chicken broth

2 tsp/10g brown sugar

1 head broccoli, cut into flowerets

¼ cauliflower, cut into flowerets

1 carrot, sliced

2 cakes thin noodles, cooked

Method

Heat butter or oil in a wok or heavy saucepan, add all seasoning ingredients, and sauté for 2–3 minutes. Add the chicken and continue sautéing for 3 minutes over high heat.

Add chicken broth and salt, and simmer until chicken is tender. Strain the brother and reserve the chicken pieces. Place rice in a rice-cooker or heavy pot, add 2½ cups/1 pint/600ml of the reserved chicken broth, and bring to the boil. Cover the pan and simmer until the rice is almost cooked and the liquid absorbed. Add the diced chicken and cook over low heat until the rice is thoroughly cooked.

Serve on a platter garnished with fried shallots and pineapple pieces.

Ingredients

2 tbsp/30ml butter or oil

1¼ lb/500g boneless chicken, cut in ½in/1cm cubes

3 cups/1¼ pints/750ml chicken broth

1 tsp/5g salt

2 cups/1lb/450g long-grain rice, washed and drained

½ small pineapple, peeled and cut into small pieces

13 shallots, peeled and minced

7 garlic cloves, peeled and minced

Seasoning

1in/2.5cm ginger, peeled and chopped

1 tsp/5g coriander

½ tsp/2.5g white peppercorns

Nasi kebuli—Chicken and Rice with Pineapple

½ tsp/2.5g cumin seed

a little freshly grated nutmeg

3in/8cm cinnamon stick

4 cardamom pods, bruised

2 cloves

1 piece lemongrass, bruised

Method

Grind the ingredients for the boemboe paste in a mortar with a pestle or chop them finely in a food processor, until you have a smooth paste.

Marinate the beef for 1-2 hours in the paste.

Heat the oil in a wok or skillet. Stir-fry the beef strips for 4-5 minutes.

Add the water, bring to the boil, add the beans, and simmer for another 3-4 minutes or until the meat is cooked through.

Empal daging—Spicy Beef Strips

Ingredients	For the boemboe paste
2 tbsp/30ml peanut oil	1 tsp/5g coriander seeds
1¼lb/500g beef, thinly sliced	4 garlic cloves, minced
½ cup4fl oz/125ml water	1 tsp/5g chopped galangal
1 bunch snake beans or long beans,	1 tsp/5g palm sugar or brown sugar
trimmed and cut into 2in/5cm pieces.	1 tbsp/15ml tamarind concentrate

Method

Crush or pound ingredients for the paste in a mortar and pestle or food processor. Heat oil in a large saucepan. Add the chops or cutlets and cook for 2-3 minutes each side or until brown. Remove and set aside.

Add paste to saucepan and cook for 1-2 minutes. Add tomatoes, water, lemongrass, and the meat. Cover and simmer for 30-40 minutes or until chops are tender and sauce has reduced.

Kambing masak—Lamb with Tomatoes

Ingredients

4 lamb chops

1¾ cups/420g/15oz canned tomatoes. chopped

½ cup water

2 potatoes, peeled and diced

1 stalk lemongrass, bruised

4 shallots, minced

2 garlic cloves, minced

4 small chili peppers, deseeded and chopped

pinch of salt

1 tbsp/15ml vegetable oil

Method

Crush or pound ingredients for paste in a mortar with pestle or in a food processor.

Chop spare ribs in half. Heat 1 tbsp/15ml oil in a wok or skillet.

Add spare ribs and stir-fry for 5–6 minutes or until ribs are golden and crisp. Remove and set aside.

Heat remaining oil and add paste. Stir-fry for 1 minute. Add coriander, cumin, pepper, soy sauce, tamarind, and sugar. Return ribs to sauce and simmer covered for 10 minutes or until ribs are cooked through.

Add a little water if sauce becomes too thick.

Ingredients

1½lb/750g pork spare ribs

1½ tbsp/20ml peanut oil

1 tsp/5g ground coriander

½ tsp ground cumin

½ tsp ground pepper

2 tbsp/30ml soy sauce

1 tbsp/15ml tamarind concentrate

Babi tulang cin—Indonesian Pork Spare Ribs

1 tsp/5g brown sugar

¼ cup/2fl oz/50ml water

For the boemboe paste

2 shallots, minced

2 garlic cloves

2 tsp/10g chopped ginger

meat

Method

Combine oil, lime juice, soy sauce, garlic, coriander and cumin.

Place lamb cutlets in a dish. Pour marinade over them and marinate for 2-3 hours.

Cook lamb cutlets on a barbecue griddle, or under the broiler for 8-10 minutes, basting and turning from time to time.

Serve with nasi goreng and peanut sauce.

Kambing panggang—Barbecued Lamb Cutlets

2 garlic cloves, crushed

1 tsp/5g ground coriander

1 tsp/5g ground cumin

Ingredients

8 lamb cutlets

2 tbsp/30ml peanut oil

nasi goreng and peanut sauce , to serve

¼ cup/2fl oz/60ml lime juice

1 tbsp/15ml soy sauce

Method

Crush or pound the shallots, garlic and shrimp paste with the peanut oil in a mortar with pestle or in a food processor.
Heat the frying oil in a wok or skillet. Stir-fry the beef for 3-4 minutes or until browned. Add the lombok chili peppers and ketjap manis. Heat the broth and dissolve the tamarind concentrate in it. Add this to the wok with the shallot-and-shrimp paste. Reduce the heat,cover the pan and simmer for around 10 minutes. Add the cubed eggplant and green onions and cook for another 5-6 minutes until the meat is well cooked and has absorbed most of the liquid of the sauce.

Ingredients

2 shallots, minced

2 garlic cloves, minced

½ tsp/2.5g terasi (shrimp paste)

2 tsp/10ml peanut oil

1 tbsp/15ml oil for frying

1lb 10oz/750g rump steak, diced

Daging asam—Beef in Tamarind

Paste

1 tbsp/15ml ketjap manis

1 tbsp/15ml tamarind concentrate

½–¾ cup/4–6fl oz/125–150ml beef broth

1 eggplant, diced

2 green onions, sliced

Method

Preheat oven to 40°F/200°C

Make two diagonal cuts on each side of the fish. Brush fish with oil and lime juice. Season with salt and place slices of lime in the fish. Wrap fish in nonstick baking paper or aluminum foil and place in a roasting pan. Bake in for 30-40 minutes or until cooked.

Heat oil in a small saucepan. Add garlic, ginger, chili pepper, and shallots and cook for 1-2 minutes. Add soy sauce, ketjap manis, and water and cook for 2-3 minutes. When fish is baked, transfer to a large serving platter and coat it with the sauce.

Ikan ketjap—Baked Fish with Spicy Soy Sauce

Ingredients

1lb 12oz/800g—1kg whole red snapper

2 tsp/10ml peanut oil

1 tbsp/15ml lime juice

pinch salt

Fish Sauce

2 tsp/10ml peanut oil

2 garlic cloves, crushed

2 tsp/10g grated ginger

1 small red chili pepper, deseeded and sliced

4 green onions, sliced

2 tbsp/30ml soy sauce

1 tbsp/15ml ketjap manis

½ cup/4fl oz/125ml water

Method

Crush or pound ingredients for the boemboe paste in a mortar and pestle or in a food processor.

Heat the frying oil a wok or skillet. Add shrimp and stir-fry for 3-4 minutes or until cooked.

Serve shrimp with Nasi Goreng or white rice.

Ingredients

Boemboe paste

3 garlic cloves, minced

2 small chili peppers, deseeded and chopped

3 tsp/15g chopped ginger

1 stalk lemongrass, chopped

1 tsp/5g ground coriander

2 tsp/10ml vegetable oil

pinch of salt

Udang goreng—Shrimp with Sambal

fish and seafood

1 tbsp/15ml frying oil

24 green (raw) shrimp, heads and

shells discarded

3

Method

Combine lime juice, turmeric, garlic, and salt to make a marinade.

Slice calamari into rings or pieces. Place squid in a dish.

Pour marinade over the calamari and marinate 2-3 hours in the refrigerator.

Dip calamari in flour and fry in hot oil until golden and crisp.

Serve with sliced chili peppers and slices of lime.

Cumi cumi goreng—Fried Calamari

Ingredients

¼ cup/2fl oz/60ml lime juice

½ tsp/2.5g ground turmeric

1 garlic clove, crushed

pinch salt

4 cups/1lb/500g calamari

⅓ cup/1½oz/45g flour

oil for frying

2 medium red chili peppers, deseeded and sliced

lime wedges

fish and seafood

Method

Prepare banana leaf by cutting into 6in/15cm squares.

Line each banana leaf with nonstick baking paper.

Combine fish, shallots, garlic, ginger, lime juice, and egg in a food processor. Process until mixture coheres into a paste.

Divide mixture evenly into 4 and place one portion in the center of each banana leaf, patting it down into a rectangle. Wrap the fish in the nonstick baking paper to make a package, seam side downward, and then fold the banana leaf the same way. Secure with cocktail sticks.

Cook the packages in a bamboo steamer for 10-15 minutes.

Serve fish with wedges of lime.

Ingredients

4 large pieces banana leaf

1lb 10oz/750g boneless white fish fillets

2 shallots, minced

2 garlic cloves, minced

2 tsp/10g chopped ginger

2 tbsp/10ml lime juice

1 egg, beaten

lime wedges to garnish

Ikan panggang—Fish in Banana Leaves

5tbsp/2½ fl oz/75 ml coconut milk

1 lime, sliced

4 lombok chili peppers, finely chopped

nonstick baking paper, cocktail sticks

fish and seafood

47

Method

Grind or pound ingredients for the paste in a mortar with a pestle or in a food processor. Brush the paste over fish fillets.

Heat the oil in a large skillet. Add fish fillets and fry for 1-2 minutes on each side. Add coconut milk, sugar, and lime juice and simmer 2-3 minutes.

Serve fish topped with green onions.

Ikan Goreng—Fried Fish

Ingredients

1 tbsp/15ml peanut oil

4 boneless fish fillets

½–¾ cup/4–6fl oz/125–150ml coconut milk

1 tsp/5g palm sugar or brown sugar

1 tbsp/15ml lime juice

4 green onions, sliced

Boemboe paste

2 garlic cloves, chopped

2 tsp/10g chopped ginger

1 stalk lemongrass, sliced

2 medium chili peppers, deseeded and sliced

2 candlenuts

½ tsp/2.5g ground turmeric

2tsp/10ml peanut oil

Grind or pound ingredients for paste in a mortar and pestle
or a food processor.

Heat oil in a wok or large skillet. Add paste a cook for
1-2 minutes. Add turmeric and coriander and cook until aromatic.

Add coconut milk, lime juice, palm sugar, and lime leaves.

Bring to the boil, add seafood, and cook until seafood is tender.

Paste

2 shallots, minced

2 cloves garlic, minced

2 tsp/10g chopped ginger

3 medium chili peppers, sliced

1 lemongrass stalk, sliced

Ikan, Udang, Cumi Cumi Kari— Seafood Curry

1 tbsp/15ml peanut oil

½ tsp/2.5g ground turmeric

1 tsp/5g ground coriander

1 cup/8fl oz/250ml coconut milk

2 tbsp/30ml lime juice

2 tsp/10g palm sugar or brown sugar

2 lime leaves, shredded

14oz/400g white fish fillets, diced

⅔ cup/5½oz/150g green shrimp, heads and shells discarded

⅔ cup/5½oz150g calamari rings

Combine oil, lime rind, lime juice, chili peppers, and garlic in a shallow dish.

Thread shrimp onto bamboo skewers and brush marinade over them.

Add calamari and brush with marinade. Leave to marinate for 30 minutes.

Cook shrimp and calamari on a barbecue plate or char grill for 5-10 minutes or until cooked.

Udang, Cumi Cumi Bakar—Marinated Barbecued Seafood

2 tbsp/30ml peanut oil

1 lime, rind grated, juice squeezed

3 chili peppers, deseeded and finely chopped

2 cloves garlic, crushed

16 large green shrimp, shelled

1cup/8oz/250g calamari rings

Heat the oil in a wok or skillet. Add chicken and cook for 4-5 minutes or until golden. Add onion, garlic, lemongrass, and ginger. Cook until onion is soft. Add coriander, turmeric, and cumin and cook until aromatic.

Add the coconut milk and curry leaves and simmer uncovered or until sauce has thickened.

Stir the coriander leaves through the mixture.

Serve with white rice.

2 tbsp/30ml vegetable oil

4 chicken thigh cutlets

1 onion, chopped

3 cloves garlic, crushed

1 piece lemongrass, finely chopped

1 tsp/5g grated ginger

Ayam Jawa—Javanese Curried Chicken

1 tsp/5g ground coriander

1 tsp/5g ground turmeric

½ tsp/2.5g ground cumin

1 cup/8fl oz/250ml coconut milk

6 curry leaves

¼ cup/2oz/60g coriander leaves (cilantro)

poultry

Place chicken in a large saucepan. Cover with water, add salt, and bring to the boil. Reduce heat, cover, and simmer for 30-35 minutes or until chicken is cooked. Remove chicken and strain liquid. Remove skin and bones from chicken and shred the flesh.

Cook noodles according to package directions. Drain and reserve.

Heat oil in a large saucepan. Add garlic, ginger and lemon grass and cook for 1-2 minutes. Add turmeric and coriander and cook until aromatic.

Add the chicken broth and lime leaves. Return the chicken to the pot and simmer for 10 minutes. Add lime juice just before serving.

Place noodles in serving bowls. Spoon over chicken soup and top with the garnishes.

Serve with wedges of lime, sambal ketjap, or sambal cuka.

Soto Ayam—Spicy Chicken Soup

2lb 12oz—3lb 5oz/1.2—1.5 kg whole chicken

3 tsp/15g salt

⅓ cup/3½oz/100g vermicelli

2 tbsp/30ml peanut oil

2 cloves garlic, crushed

2 tsp/10g grated ginger

1 stick lemongrass, white part finely chopped, (tie top part of lemon grass)

1 tsp/5g turmeric

2 tsp/10g ground coriander

8 cups/3½ pints/2 l chicken broth

2 kaffir lime leaves, thinly sliced

1 lime, juice squeezed

Garnishes

4 green shallots, sliced

1 cup/8oz/250g beansprouts, trimmed

2 hard-boiled eggs, quartered

2 potatoes, cooked and sliced

Preheat oven to 425°F/220°C

Combine soy sauce, tamarind, oil, ginger, garlic, and coriander. Pour marinade over duck and leave to marinate for 2-3 hours.

Heat oil in a skillet. Add duck and cook for 1–2 minutes or until golden and crisp. Place duck on a rack over a roasting pan and cook for 15-18 minutes. Slice duck and serve with salad greens.

2 tbsp/30ml soy sauce

1 tbsp/15ml tamarind concentrate

1 tbsp/15ml peanut oil

1 tsp/5g grated ginger

1 clove garlic crushed

1 tsp/5g ground coriander

Bebek Goreng—Crispy Fried Duck

4 duck breasts

¼ cup/2fl oz/60ml peanut oil, for frying

Heat oil in a large saucepan. Add chicken and cook for 4–5 minutes or until golden. Add shallots, garlic, and ginger. Cook until shallots are soft. Add turmeric, coriander, cumin, and laos powder. Cook until aromatic.

Add coconut milk, chicken broth, sambal oelek, lemongrass, and salam leaves. Bring to the boil. Add vegetables and cook for 10-15 minutes or until vegetables are tender.

Serve with white rice.

Ayam Jawa Sayur—Javanese Chicken and Vegetables

2 tbsp/30ml peanut oil

6 chicken thighs, boned

3 shallots, sliced

2 cloves garlic, crushed

2 tsp/10g grated ginger

1 tsp/5g ground turmeric

1 tsp ground coriander

1 tsp ground cumin

1 tsp galangal powder

1 cup/8fl oz/250ml coconut milk

¾ cup/6fl oz/175ml chicken broth

2 tsp/10g sambal oelek

1 stalk lemon grass, bruised

2 salam leaves or 4 curry leaves

1 carrot, sliced

2 potatoes, diced

⅓ cup/3½ oz/100g green beans, sliced

Crush or pound ingredients for the paste in a mortar with a pestle or in a food processor.

Heat oil in a large saucepan. Add chicken and cook until golden. Remove chicken and set aside.

Add onions and cook for 3-4 minutes or until brown. Add paste and cook for 1-2 minutes. Add coriander, cumin, and laos powder and cook until aromatic.

Add coconut cream, milk, kaffir lime leaves, and chicken. Bring to the boil, reduce heat and simmer for 20-30 minutes or until chicken is tender and liquid has reduced.

Opor-Ayam—Chicken in Coconut Milk

2 tbsp/20ml peanut oil

8 chicken pieces

Paste

2 onions, sliced

2 cloves garlic

2 tsp/10g ground coriander

2 tsp/10g chopped ginger

1 tsp/5g ground cumin

1 tsp/5g terasi (shrimp paste)

pinch of laos powder

3 candlenuts

1½ cups/12oz/350g creamed coconut

1 small red chili, deseeded

1½ cups/12fl oz/350ml coconut milk

½ tsp/2.5g salt

2 kaffir lime leaves, thinly sliced

Preheat oven to 400°F/200°C.

Place chicken in a large saucepan and cover with water. Bring to the boil and simmer for 15-20 minutes. Remove chicken from water and pat dry with paper towels.

Heat margarine in a small saucepan. Add garlic and cook for 1—2 minutes. Add ketjap manis, tamarind, and sambal oelek. Bring to the boil. Remove from heat and brush over the sauce over the chicken.

Place the chicken on a rack over a roasting pan. Cover lightly with aluminum foil and bake in a preheated oven for 1 hour or until cooked, basting at least every 15 minutes.

Cut chicken into serving pieces and serve with lime wedges.

Ayam Panggang Pedis—Roast Spiced Chicken

3lb 5oz/1.5 kg chicken

3 tbsp/45g margarine

2 cloves garlic, crushed

2 tbsp/30ml ketjap manis

2 tbsp/30ml tamarind concentrate

2—3 tsp/10—15ml sambal oelek

wedges of lime to serve

Combine garlic, ginger, lemongrass, ketjap manis, soy sauce, sambal oelek, and sesame oil in a shallow dish.

Add chicken and coat well in marinade. Leave to marinate for 1-2 hours.

Heat oil in a wok or skillet. Add chicken, reserving the marinade, and stir-fry for 4-5 minutes or until golden.

Add marinade and snow peas and bamboo shoots and stir-fry for 2-3 minutes or until snow peas are cooked.

Add a little water if the sauce becomes too thick.

2 cloves garlic, crushed

2 tsp/10g ginger, chopped

1 stalk lemongrass, finely chopped

1 tbsp/15ml ketjap manis

1 tsp/5ml sambal oelek

2 tsp/10ml sesame oil

Marinated Chicken with Snow Peas

1¼lb/500g chicken breasts, halved

1 tbsp/15ml peanut oil

⅔ cup/5½oz/150g snow peas, trimmed and halved

1cup/8oz/230g canned bamboo shoots, drained

Heat oil in a wok or frying pan. Add sesame oil, garlic, shallots and beans.

Stir-fry for 2-3 minutes. Add soy sauce and water and cook for 3-4 minutes or until beans are just cooked.

Stir the beansprouts and peanuts into the mixture.

Buncis ketjap—Green Beans with Soy Sauce

1 tbsp/15ml peanut oil

1 tsp/5ml sesame oil

1 clove garlic, crushed

2 shallots, sliced

10½oz/300g green beans, trimmed and halved

2 tbsp/20ml soy sauce

2 tbsp/30ml water

1 cup/8oz/250g beansprouts, trimmed

⅓ cup/3½oz/100g roasted peanuts, chopped

Arrange cooked vegetables on a large serving platter and serve with peanut sauce and sambals.

Gado-Gado—Vegetables with Peanut Sauce

2 large potatoes, peeled and cooked

⅔cup/5½oz/150g long beans, blanched

2 carrots, sliced and blanched

1/3 cup/3½oz/100g tofu

1/3 cup/3½oz/100g peanut sauce

1/3 cup/3½oz/100g ketjap manis

Heat oil in a large saucepan. Add onion and cook for 2–3 minutes or until soft.

Add garlic, terasi, and candlenuts and cook for 1 minute.

Add coconut milk, chicken broth, sambal oelek, and lemongrass.

Bring to the boil. Add broccoli and cauliflower. Cover and simmer for 4 minutes.

Add zucchini and beans and continue to cook for 3-4 minutes or until vegetables are barely tender.

Remove lemongrass just before serving.

Sayur Lodeh—Vegetables in Coconut Milk

1 tbsp/15ml peanut oil

1 onion, sliced

2 cloves garlic, crushed

1 tsp/5g terasi, crushed

2 candlenuts, crushed

½ cup/4fl oz/125ml coconut milk

1 cup/8fl oz/250ml chicken broth

1 tsp/5ml sambal oelek

1 stalk lemongrass, bruised

1 head broccoli, cut into flowerets

¼ cauliflower, cut into flowerets

1 large zucchini, halved and sliced

⅔ cup/5½oz/150g green beans, sliced

vegetables

75

Heat the oil in a wok or frying pan. Cook tempeh in batches until golden and crisp. Remove and set aside.

Heat the peanut oil and add garlic and terasi.

Cook for 30 seconds. Add tamarind, soy sauce, sugar, water and tempeh.

Cook until sauce has reduced.

Garnish with sliced green shallots.

½ cup/4fl oz/125ml vegetable oil for frying

1¼ cups/10½oz/300g tempeh, cut into thin strips

2 tsp/10ml peanut oil

2 cloves garlic, crushed

¼ tsp/1.25g terasi, crushed

2 tbsp/30ml tamarind concentrate

Sambal Goreng Tempeh—Spicy Fried Tempeh

1 tbsp/15ml soy sauce

1–2 tsp/5–10g palm sugar or brown sugar

1-2 tbsp/15-30ml water

2 green shallots, sliced

vegetables

Brush eggplant slices with half the oil. Heat a large nonstick skillet. Add eggplant and cook 1-2 minutes each side until golden. Remove and set aside.

Heat remaining oil. Add onions and cook for 4-5 minutes or until golden. Add garlic, chili peppers, coriander, tamarind, and sugar.

Return eggplant to pan and cook until sauce reduces.

Terong Goreng—Spicy Fried Eggplant

¼ cup/2fl oz/60ml peanut oil

2 eggplant, cut into ½ inch/1cm thick slices

2 onions, sliced

2 cloves garlic, crushed

2 small chili peppers, deseeded and finely chopped

1 tsp/5g ground coriander

2 tbsp/10ml tamarind concentrate

1 tsp/5g palm sugar or brown sugar

Grind or pound ingredients for paste in a mortar with a pestle or in a food processor. If using a food processor you may need to add a little oil.

Heat oil in a wok or skillet. Add paste and cook for 1–2 minutes. Add broth and lemongrass. Bring to the boil.

Add beans and cook for 8-10 minutes or until beans are tender.

Sambal Buncis—Spicy Long Beans

Paste

4 small red chili peppers, deseeded
and sliced

2 shallots, chopped

2 tsp/10g chopped ginger

2 tsp/10g chopped garlic

2 tsp/10ml peanut oil

1 cup/8fl oz/250ml chicken broth

1 stalk lemongrass, bruised

1 cup/8oz/250g runner beans, trimmed

Heat the oil in a wok or skillet. Add the tofu and cook until golden and crisp. Remove and set aside.

Heat the peanut oil and add ginger and chili peppers. Stir-fry for 1—2 minutes. Add soy sauce, water, sugar, tofu, and snow peas. Stir-fry for 2-3 minutes or until snow peas are tender. Stir in the beansprouts and serve.

Tahu Goreng ketjap—Fried Bean Curd in Soy Sauce

½ cup/4fl oz/125ml vegetable oil for frying

1 cup/8oz/250g tofu, diced

2 tsp/10ml peanut oil

2 tsp/10g grated ginger

2 medium chili peppers, deseeded and sliced

¼ cup/2 fl oz/60ml soy sauce

1—2 tbsp/15—30ml water

2 tsp/10g palm sugar or brown sugar

1 cup/7oz/200g snow peas, trimmed and halved

1 cup7oz/200g beansprouts, trimmed

Crush or pound ingredients for paste in a mortar with a pestle or in a food processor. If using a food processor, you may need to add a little oil.

Heat the oil in a wok or saucepan. Add paste and laos powder and cook for 1 minute. Add chicken broth, tamarind, water, and vegetables.

Bring to the boil and cook for 6-8 minutes or until vegetables are tender.

Sayur Asam—Sweet-and-sour Vegetables

Ingredients

1 tbsp/15ml peanut oil	1 cup/8oz/250g shredded cabbage
1 tsp/5ml laos powder	⅓ cup/5½oz/100g green beans
1–1½ cups/8–12fl oz/250–350ml chicken broth	**Paste**
2 tbsp/30ml tamarind concentrate	2 shallots, minced
1 tsp/5g palm sugar or brown sugar	2 cloves garlic
1 zucchini, sliced	2 small chili peppers, deseeded and chopped
1 eggplant, diced	½ tsp/2.5g terasi

Preheat oven to 375°F/180°C. Lightly grease a 8in/20cm cake pan and line the bottom with nonstick baking paper. Combine butter and sugar in a mixing bowl. Cream butter and sugar together until light and fluffy. Add eggs one at a time, beating well after each addition.

Grind bananas in a food processor with the lemon juice. Process until very mushy. Stir bananas into the mixture. Add flour, baking soda, cinnamon and coconut, stirring well until fully incorporated

Spoon mixture into prepared cake pan and bake in the preheated oven for 40-45 minutes. Test for doneness by inserting a toothpick into the center of the cake; if it comes out clean, the cake is baked.

Leave cake to cool for 10-15 minutes then turn out onto a cake rack.

Cut into wedges and serve with cream or ice cream.

½ cup/4oz/125g butter, at room temperature

1 cup/8oz/250g caster sugar

2 eggs

3 bananas

½ cup/4fl oz/125ml lemon juice

1½ cups/6oz/175g self-rising flour

½ tsp/2.5g baking soda

½ tsp/2.5g ground cinnamon

1 cup/8oz/250g unsweetened shredded coconut

Banana and Coconut Cake

Tip

If you cannot find self-rising flour, use all-purpose

flour and add 1 tsp/5g baking powder.

desserts

87

Combine flour, cinnamon, sugar and water in a mixing bowl.

Whisk mixture until you have a smooth batter..

Cut bananas in half lengthwise and then into pieces. Dip banana banana pieces in batter.

Heat the frying oil in a wok or skillet add bananas. Fry until golden and crisp.

Pisang Goreng—Banana Fritters

¾ cup/3oz/85g rice flour

1 tsp/5g ground cinnamon

1 tsp/5g superfine (caster) sugar

¼—⅓ cup/2—3½ fl oz/50—100 ml water

3 bananas, peeled

vegetable oil for frying

Rinse rice under cold running water for

1-2 minutes or until water is clear.

Combine rice, water, and pandanus leaves

in a large saucepan. Bring to the boil and

simmer over low heat for 40 minutes.

Add syrup and cook for a further 10 minutes

or until rice is tender and liquid has been absorbed.

Serve pudding with coconut milk or ice cream.

To make the syrup, combine sugar and water

in a small saucepan. Bring to the boil

and simmer for 8-10 minutes, or until thickened.

Ingredients

1½ cups/12oz/350g black glutinous rice

4–4½ cups/1¾–2 pints/1 l–1.125 l water

2 pandanus leaves

½ cup/4fl oz/125ml palm sugar syrup

coconut milk or ice cream to serve

Bubuh Injin—Black Rice Pudding

Palm Sugar Syrup

1 cup/8oz/250g grated palm sugar or piloncillo,

or brown sugar

½ cup/4 fl oz/125ml water

Combine the flour and sugar in a mixing bowl. Add the eggs and milk and whisk mixture until smooth.

Heat a skillet. Spray or sprinkle with a little oil, and add enough of the mixture to make a thin pancake. Cook the pancakes for 1-2 minutes each side.

Combine sugar, water, and pandanus leaf in a saucepan. Bring to the boil and simmer over low heat, and stir until sugar dissolves. Add coconut and cook until all the liquid has been absorbed.

Place one tablespoonful of the coconut mixture on each pancake and roll it up like a cigar. Serve pancakes with ice cream.

Dadar Gulang—Coconut Pancakes

½ cup/2oz/60g all-purpose flour

1 tbsp/15g superfine sugar

2 eggs, lightly beaten

¾ cup/6fl oz/175ml milk or coconut milk

oil spray for cooking

1 cup/8oz/250g grated palm sugar or brown sugar

½ cup/4fl oz/125ml water

1 pandanus leaf

1 cup unsweetened shredded coconut

Combine sugar, water, lime rind and juice in a small saucepan. Bring to the boil and simmer over low heat for 8-10 minutes. Add tamarind and chili peppers and stir to combine.

Combine ingredients for fruit in a serving bowl. Pour the syrup over the fruits and toss to mix well.

Ingredients

½ pineapple, diced

1 mango, diced

1 papaya, diced

1 apple, cored and diced

1 cucumber, diced

12 rambutans or lychees, peeled and pitted

Rujak—Fruit Salad in Lime Syrup

Syrup

1 cup/8oz/250g grated palm sugar,

piloncillo, or brown sugar

⅓ cup/3½fl oz/100ml water

1 lime, rind thinly paired, juice squeezed

1 tbsp/15ml tamarind concentrate

2 medium chili peppers, deseeded and

finely sliced

Ayam Bali—Balinese -style Fried Chicken 62

Ayam Goreng —Spicy Chicken Drumettes 16

Ayam Jawa—Javanese Curried Chicken 54

Ayam Jawa Sayur— Javanese Chicken and
Vegetables 60

Ayam Panggang Pedis — Roast Spiced
Chicken 66

Babi Tulang Cin—Indonesian Pork
Spare Ribs 34

Bami Goreng— Fried Noodles 20

Banana and Coconut Cake 86

Bebek Goreng—Crispy Fried Duck 58

Begedel Daging—Beef Croquettes 8

Bubuh Injin—Black Rice Pudding 90

Buncis Ketjap—Green Beans with
Soy Sauce 70

Cumi Cumi Goreng—Fried Calamari 44

Dadar Gulang—Coconut Pancakes 92

Daging Asam—Beef in Tamarind 38

Empal Daging—Spicy Beef Strips 28

Gado-Gado—Vegetables with
Peanut Sauce 72

Ikan Goreng—Fried Fish 48

Ikan Ketjap—Baked Fish with
Spicy Soy Sauce 40

Ikan Panggang— Fish in Banana Leaves 46

Ikan, Udang, Cumi Cumi Kari—
Seafood Curry 50

Kambing Masak—Lamb with Tomatoes 32

Kambing Panggang—Barbecued Lamb
Cutlets 36

Marinated Chicken with Snow Peas 68

Nasi Goreng—Fried Rice 18

Nasi Kebuli—Chicken and Rice with
Pineapple 26

Nasi Kuning—Yellow Rice 22

Opor-Ayam—Chicken in Coconut Milk 64

Perkedel Ikan—Spicy Fish Fritters 14

Perkedel Jagung—Corn Fritters 10

Pisang Goreng— Banana Fritters 88

Rempah Daging—Spicy Meatballs 12

Rendang Daging—Dry Fried Beef Curry 30

Rujak—Fruit Salad in Lime Syrup 94

Index

Sambal Buncis— Spicy Long Beans 80

Sambal Goreng Tempeh—Spicy
Fried Tempeh 76

Sayur Asam—Sweet-and- sour Vegetables 84

Sayur Kari—Vegetables and
Noodles in Curry 24

Sayur Lodeh—Vegetables in Coconut Milk 74

Soto Ayam—Spicy Chicken Soup 56

Tahu Goreng ketjap—Fried Bean Curd in
Soy Sauce 82

Terong Goreng—Spicy Fried Eggplant 78

Udang Goreng—Shrimp with Sambal 42

Udang, Cumi Cumi Bakar—Marinated
Barbecued Seafood 52